Contents

In Alphabetical Order By Song Title

785.85 DEC

Published 2000

Production: Miranda Steel
Cover design: The London Advertising Partnership

KT-572-254

IMP
International MUSIC Publications

International Music Publications Limited
Griffin House 161 Hammersmith Road London W6 8BS

Contents

In Alphabetical Order By Film Followed By Song Title

Published 2000

Production: Miranda Steel
Cover design: The London Advertising Partnership

IMP

International
MUSIC
Publications

International Music Publications Limited
Griffin House 161 Hammersmith Road London W6 8BS

BEAUTIFUL STRANGER

from

"Austin Powers: The Spy Who Shagged Me"

Words and Music by
Madonna Ciccone and William Orbit

%% *Bridge:*

1. I looked in - to your_____ eyes, and my world_____
2. I looked in - to your_____ face, my heart was
3. I looked in - to your_____ eyes, and my world_____

_____ danc-in' all came tum - bl - ing down._____
came tum - bl - ing o - ver the place._____
_____ came tum - bl - ing down._____

You're the dev - il in dis - guise. That's why I'm
I'd like to change my point of view, if I could
You're the dev - il in dis - guise. That's why I'm

sing - ing this song._____
just for - get a - bout you._____
sing - ing this song_____ to you._____

Chorus:

BECAUSE YOU LOVED ME

from

"Up Close And Personal"

Words and Music by Diane Warren

BRAVEHEART

Theme from

"Braveheart"

Music by James Horner

BOHEMIAN RHAPSODY
from
"Wayne's World"

Words and Music by Freddie Mercury

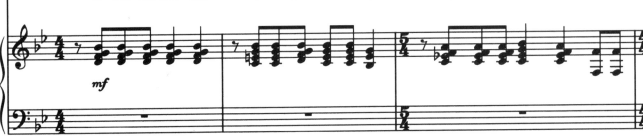

Slowly

Is this the real life? Is this just fan - ta - sy? Caught in a land - slide, no es -

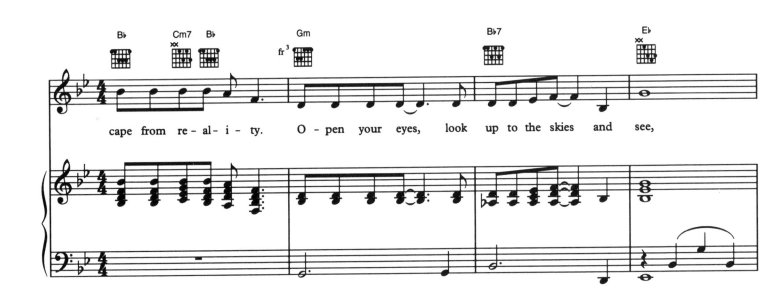

cape from re - al - i - ty. O - pen your eyes, look up to the skies and see,

I'm just a poor boy, I need no sym - pa - thy, be - cause I'm eas - y come, eas - y go,

will not let you go. Let him go! — Bis - mil - lah! We will not let you go. Let him go!

— Bis - mil - lah! We will not let you go. Let me go! — Will not let you go. Let me go!

Will not let you go. — Ah. Let me go. — No, no, no, no, no, no, no, Oh ma - ma

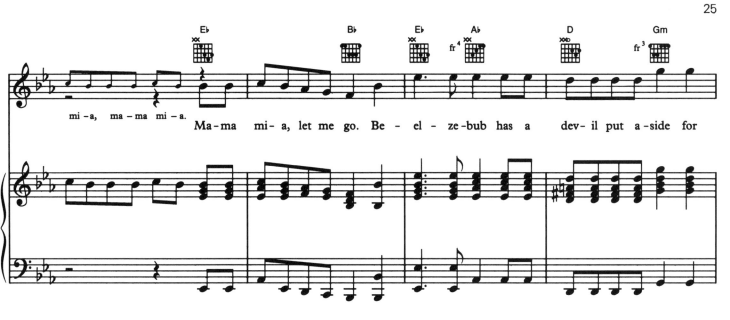

mi –a, ma –ma mi –a. Ma –ma mi– a, let me go. Be – el – ze –bub has a dev– il put a –side for

me, for me, for me.

instrumental solo

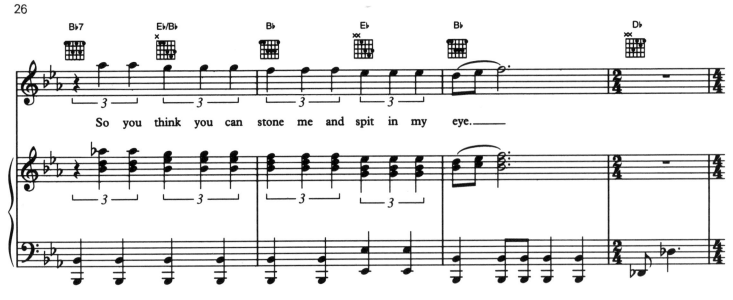

So you think you can stone me and spit in my eye.___

So you think you can love me and leave me to die.___ Oh,___

ba - by,___ can't do this to me, ba - by,___ just got - ta get out,

just got-ta get right out-ta here.

instrumental solo

poco a poco ritard. e dim.

slowly, a tempo

DUEL OF THE FATES

from

"Star Wars Episode 1: The Phantom Menace"

Music by John Williams

Maestoso, with great force

Kor - ah,_____ Mah - tah._____ Kor - ah,_____ Rah-tah - mah._____

Allegro ♩ = 152

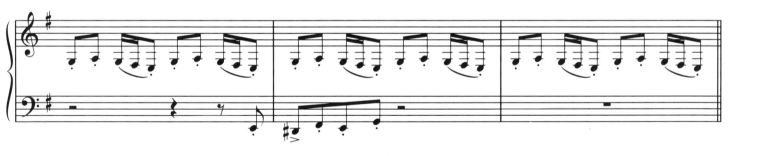

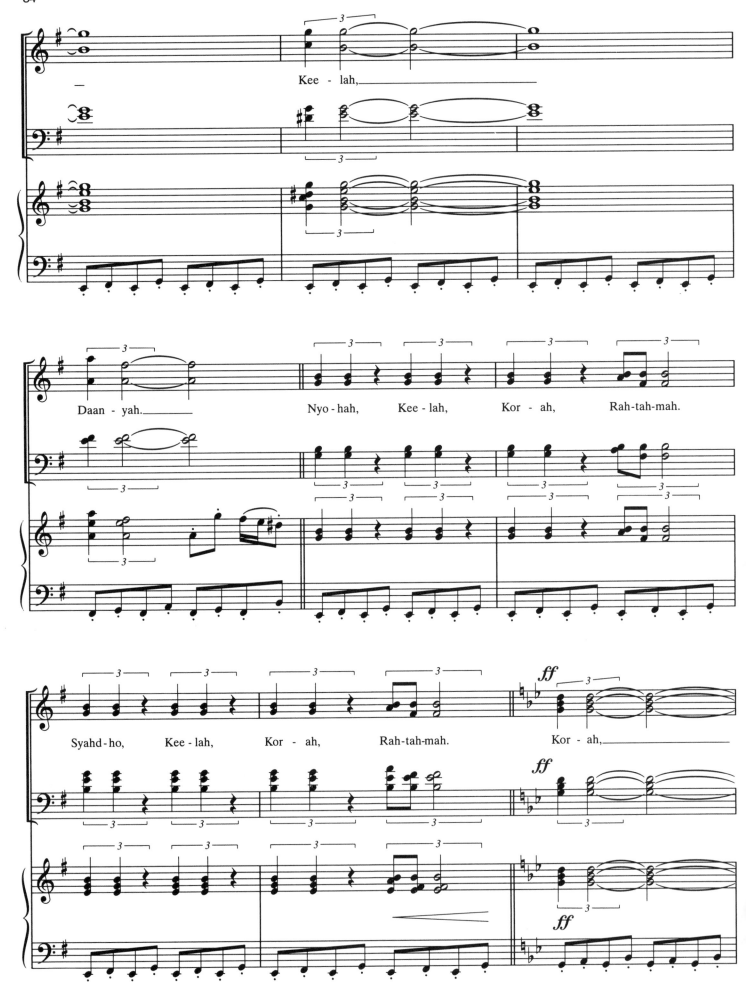

EXHALE (SHOOP SHOOP)

from

"Waiting To Exhale"

Words and Music by Kenny Edmonds

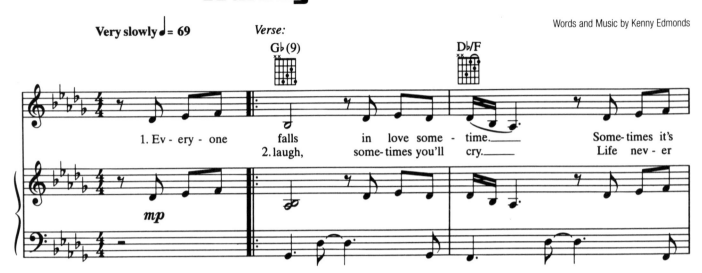

Bridge:

Hearts are of-ten bro-ken when there are words___ un-spo-ken.

In your soul_ there's an-swers to___ your prayers._____ If you're

search-ing for a place_you know, a fa-mil-iar face, some-where to go,_____ you should

look in-side your-self, you're half-way there.___ 2. Some-times you'll

Chorus:

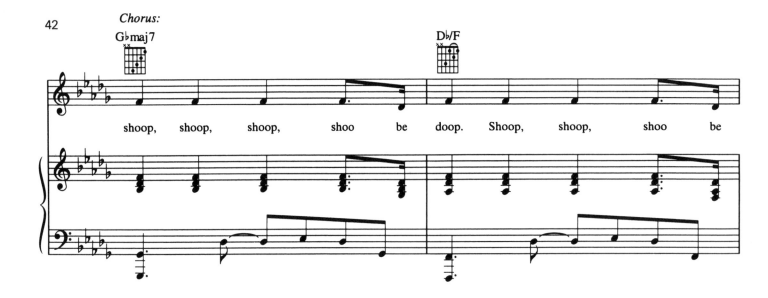

shoop, shoop, shoop, shoo be doop. Shoop, shoop, shoo be

doop. Shoop, shoop, shoo be doop. Shoop, shoop, shoo be doop. Shoop, shoop, shoo be

doop. Shoop, shoop, shoo be doop. Shoop, shoop, shoo be doop.

(EVERYTHING I DO) I DO IT FOR YOU

from

"Robin Hood, Prince Of Thieves"

Words and Music by Bryan Adams,
Robert John 'Mutt' Lange and Michael Kamen

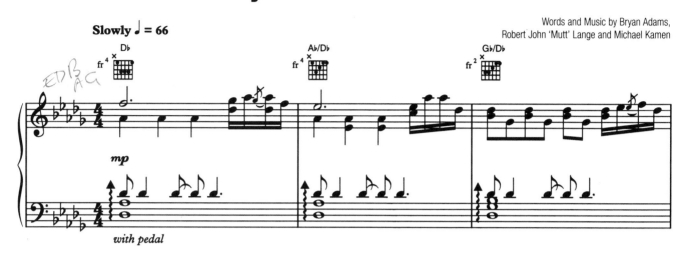

1. Look in-to my eyes,_____ you will see_____ what you mean to____ me. Search your heart, search your

(instrumental solo . . .

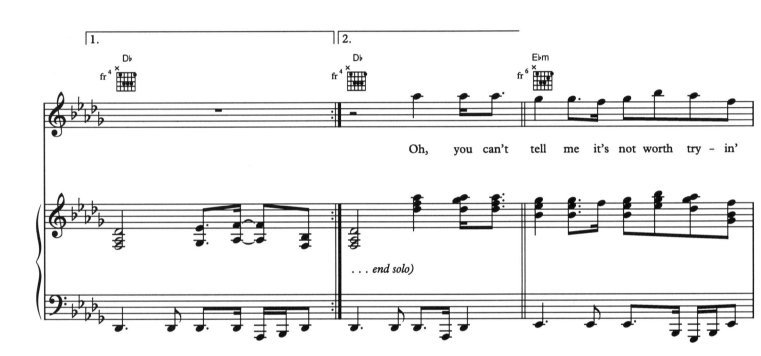

1.

2.

... end solo)

Oh, you can't tell me it's not worth try – in'

for. I can't help— it, there's no-thing I want more. Yeah, I would

cresc. *f*

HOW DO I LIVE

from

"Con Air"

Words and Music by Diane Warren

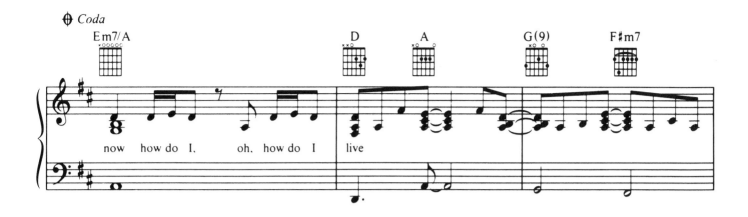

now how do I, oh, how do I live

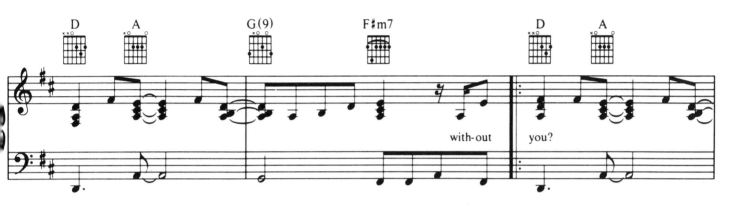

with-out you?

Repeat ad lib. and fade
(vocal 1st time only)

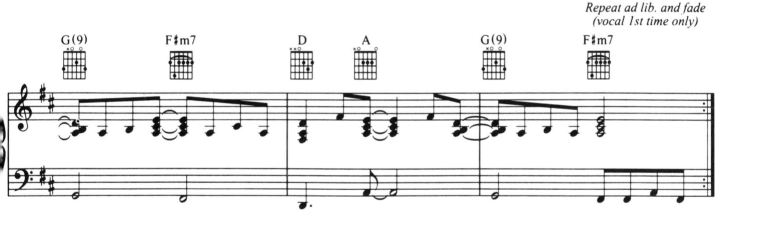

Verse 2:
Without you, there'd be no sun in my sky,
There would be no love in my life,
There'd be no world left for me.
And I, baby, I don't know what I would do,
I'd be lost if I lost you.
If you ever leave,
Baby, you would take away everything real in my life.
And tell me now...
(To Chorus:)

I WILL ALWAYS LOVE YOU
from
"The Bodyguard"

Words and Music by Dolly Parton

Verse 3: Instrumental solo

Verse 4:
I hope life treats you kind
And I hope you have all you've dreamed of.
And I wish to you, joy and happiness.
But above all this, I wish you love.
(To Chorus:)

I DON'T WANT TO MISS A THING
from
"Armageddon"

Words and Music by Diane Warren

miss you, ba - by, and I don't wan-na miss a thing.___ 'Coz e - ven when I dream of you,___

the sweet-est dream would nev - er do.___ I'd still miss you, ba - by, and I don't wan-na miss a thing.___

Repeat ad lib. and fade

IN ALL THE RIGHT PLACES
from
"Indecent Proposal"

Words by Lisa Stansfield
Music by John Barry

Moderate rock ♩ = 92

If you take me straight to heav - en, I could nev - er fall.

'Cause lov-ing you is what I'm made for, I'd glad - ly give my all - in - all.

It does - n't mat - ter where I am, as long as I'm with you.

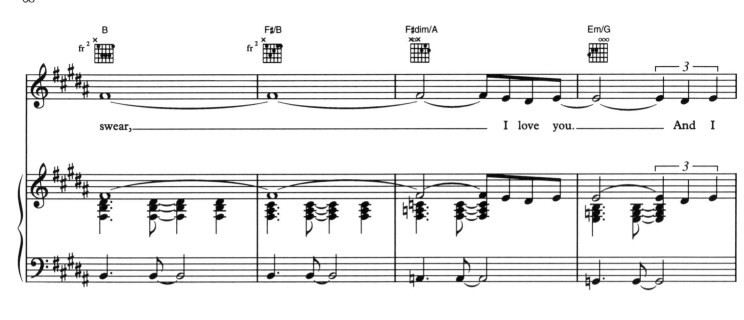

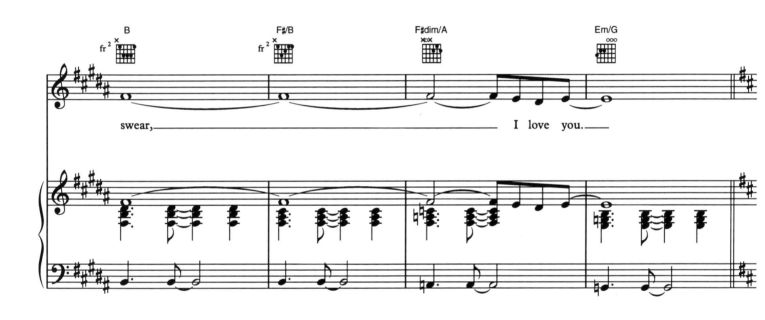

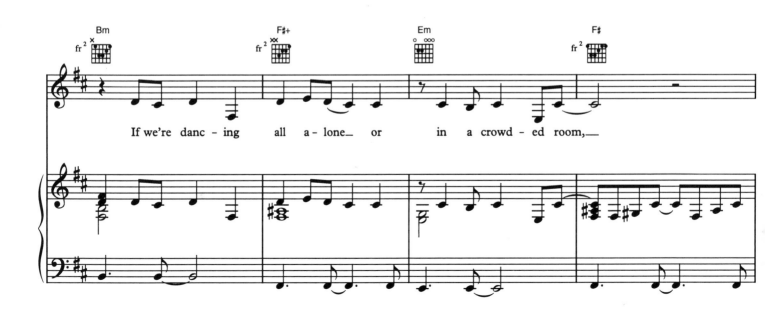

In all_____ the right plac-es, it's feel-in' so good

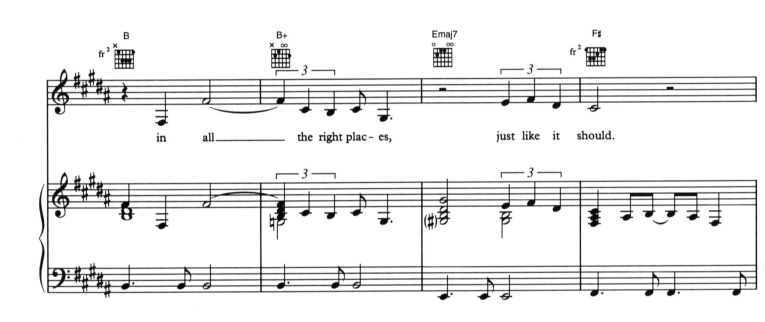

in all_____ the right plac-es, just like it should.

In times_____ nev-er wast-ed when it's ours_ to kill,

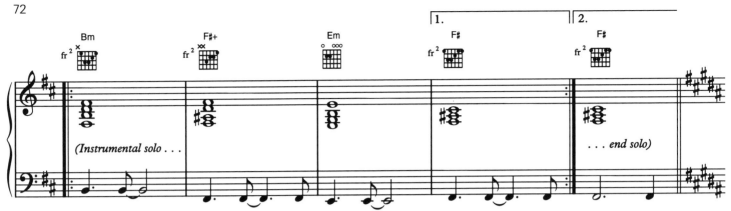

(Instrumental solo . . .   . . . end solo)

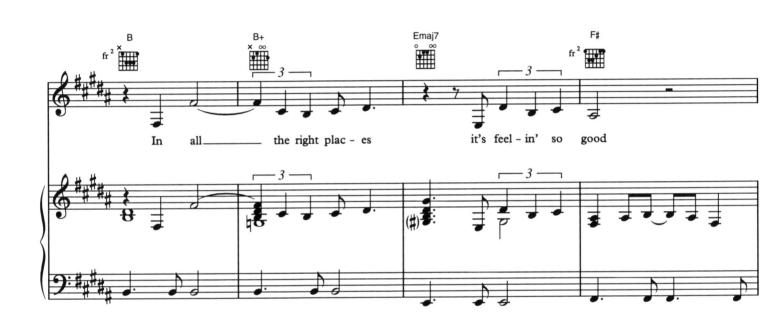

In all_____ the right plac - es   it's feel - in' so good

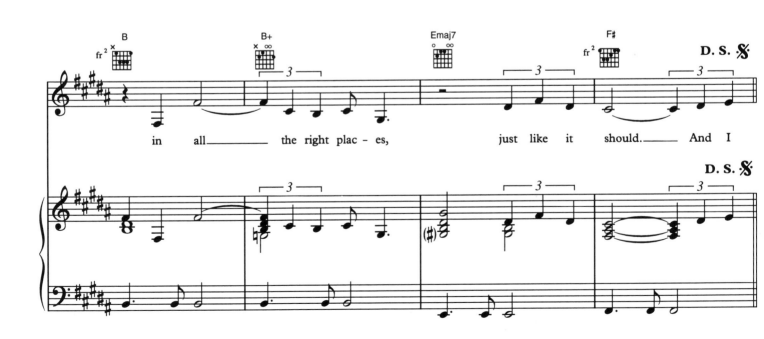

in all_____ the right plac - es,   just like it   should._____ And I

D. S. 𝄋

MAKE SOMEONE HAPPY

from

"Sleepless In Seattle"

Words by Betty Comden and Adolph Green
Music by Jule Styne

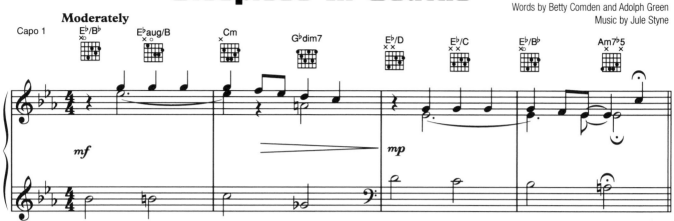

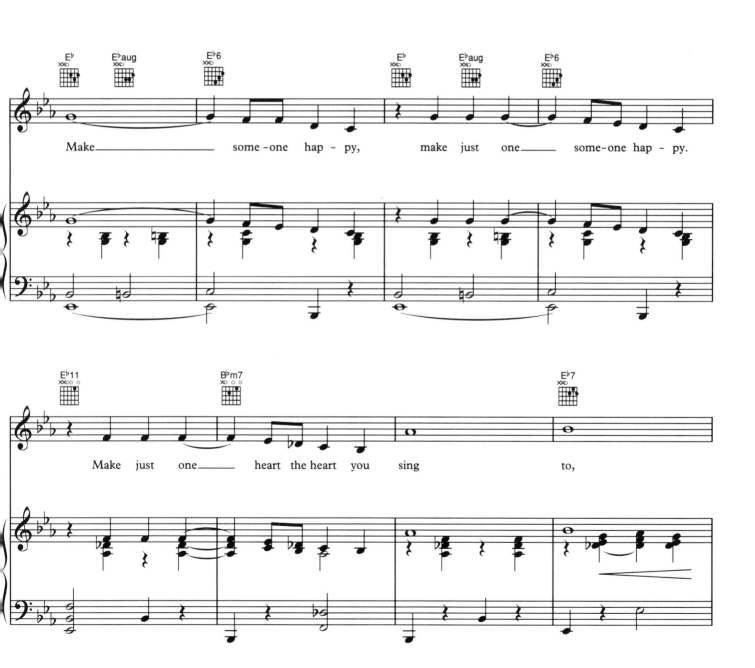

KISS FROM A ROSE

from

"Batman Returns"

Words and Music by Seal

MUSTANG SALLY

from

"The Commitments"

Words and Music by Bonny Rice

Verse 2:
I bought you a brand new Mustang
It was a nineteen sixty-five
Now you come around, signifying a woman
Girl, you won't, you won't let me ride
Mustang Sally, now baby
Guess you better slow that Mustang down
You been runnin' all over town
Oh, guess you gotta put your flat feet on the ground

MY GIRL

Theme from

"My Girl"

Words and Music by
Ronald White and William Robinson

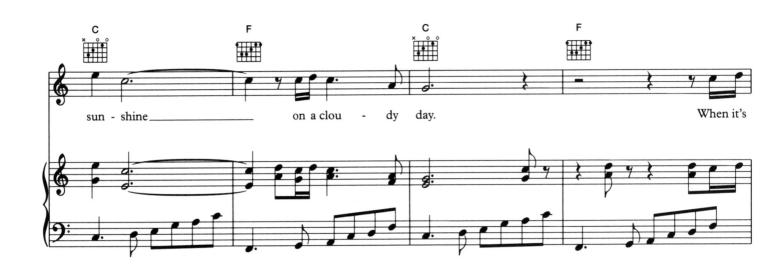

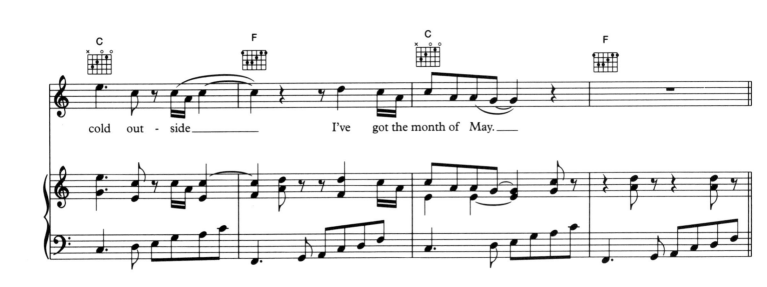

CODA

My girl!

I don't

need no _ mon - ey, _ for - tune or fame. _ I got

MY HEART WILL GO ON

Love theme from

"Titanic"

Words by Will Jennings
Music by James Horner

MY GUY
from
"Sister Act"

Words and Music by William Robinson

No-thing you could say could tear— me a-way from my— guy,—
No-thing you could do could make— me un-true to my— guy,—

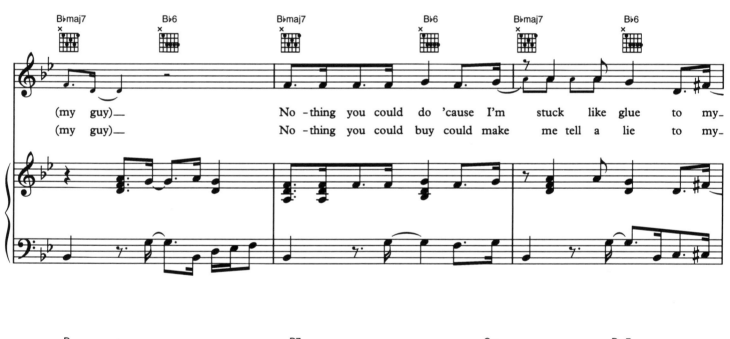

(my guy)— No-thing you could do 'cause I'm stuck like glue to my—
(my guy)— No-thing you could buy could make me tell a lie to my—

— guy.— (My guy)— I'm stick-ing to my guy like a
— guy.— (My guy)— I gave my guy my

my o-pin-ion is he's the cream of the crop; as a mat-ter of taste to

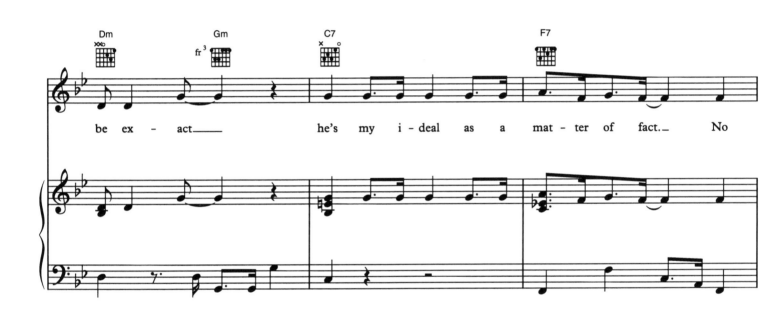

be ex - act___ he's my i-deal as a mat-ter of fact.___ No

mus-cle bound man could take my hand___ from my___ guy.___ (My guy.) No

take me a-way from my___ guy.___

D. %: al coda

No

D. %: al coda

Coda

repeat and fade

man to-day who could take me a-way from my___ guy.___ (What you say? Tell me more.) There's not a

repeat and fade

THE SHOOP SHOOP SONG (IT'S IN HIS KISS)

from

"Mermaids"

Words and Music by Rudy Clark

kiss. That's where it is._____ (Is it is._____ It's in his kiss. That's where it

is. Kiss him_____ and squeeze him tight___ and find out what you want to

know._____ Prom - ise love,_ if it real - ly is,_____ it's there in his

WHEN YOU SAY NOTHING AT ALL

from

"Notting Hill"

Words and Music by
Paul Overstreet and Don Schlitz

1. It's a-maz-ing how you can speak right___ to my heart,
(Verse 2 see block lyric)

with - out say - ing a word

smile on your face lets me know — that you need — me. There's a truth in your eyes say-ing you'll

— nev - er leave — me. The touch of your hand say's you'll catch —

The

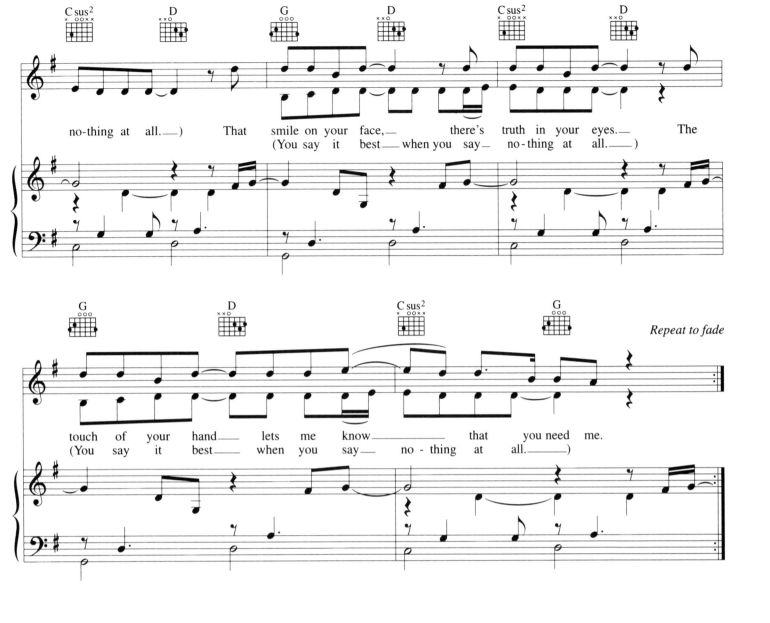

Verse 2:
All day long I can hear people talking out loud
But when you hold me you drown out the crowd
Try as they may they can never defy
What's been said between your heart and mine.

The smile on your face *etc.*

YOU SEXY THING
from
"The Full Monty"

Words and Music by
Erroll Brown and Tony Wilson

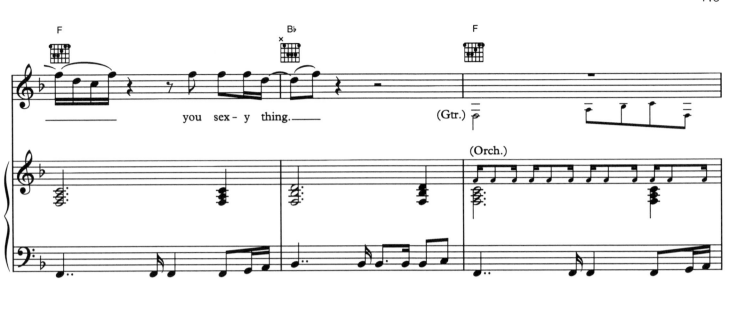

you sex-y thing.___ (Gtr.)

(Orch.)

Where did you come from ba - - by?
Where did you come from an - - gel?

How did you know___ I
How did you know___ I'd

you sex - y, you sex - y thing___
you sex - y,

you

1.

yes - ter - day___ I was one of the lone - ly peo - ple. Now you're ly - ing close to me

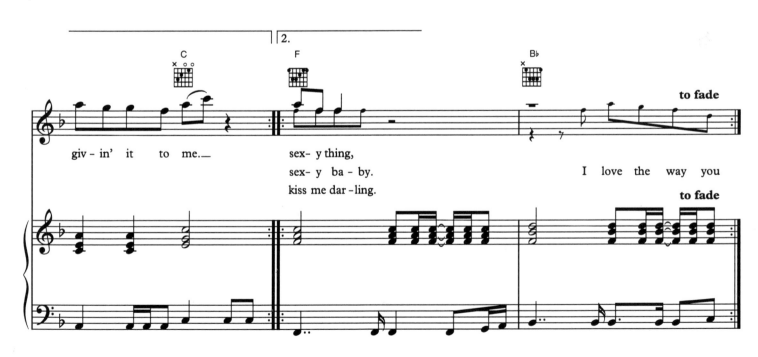

2.

giv - in' it to me.___
sex - y thing,
sex - y ba - by.
kiss me dar - ling.

I love the way you

to fade